MINOR SECRETS
Billie Chernicoff

BSE

ISBN: 978-09-997028-7-1

BSE Books are distributed by
  Small Press Distribution
  1341 Seventh Street
  Berkeley, CA 94710
  orders@spdbooks.org | www.spdbooks.org
  1-800-869-7553

BSE Books can also be purchased at
www.blacksquareeditions.org and www.hyperallergic.com

Contributions to BSE can be made to
  Off the Park Press, Inc.
  976 Kensington Ave.
  Plainfield, NJ 07060
  (Please make checks payable to Off the Park Press, Inc.)

To contact the Press please write:
  Black Square Editions
  1200 Broadway, Suite 3C
  New York, NY 10001

An independent subsidary of Off the Park Press, Inc.

Member of CLMP.

Publisher: John Yau
Editors: Ronna Lebo and Boni Joi
Design & composition: Shanna Compton

Cover art: "Self with Snuff Bottles," © Aubrey Levinthal, 2019. Oil on panel, 12 x
12 inches. By permission of Monya Rowe Gallery.

for my brothers, the swans

EVERYTHING IS DIFFERENT from what you think,
   from what I think,
   the flag still flutters,

   the little secrets are still secret,
   they still throw shadows, on this
   you live, I live, we live.

                                    —Paul Celan

The Major Arcana (or *big secrets*) of the Tarot
embody the great archetypal energies that shape
the lives of all human beings. The Minor Arcana
(or *little secrets*) represent the particulars of our
selves and our lives, the inner and outer events we
create with our own quotidian deeds and desires.
With Tarot, of course, there are always exceptions.
Sometimes the Major Arcana show us something
very specific, while the Minor Arcana take on a
life of their own.

                                    —Madame Lulu

CONTENTS

A SAIL ON LAKE ST. CLAIR

... in the unsayable, where the lie takes refuge, that dream caught in the act, sole love of humans.
—Louis-Ferdinand Céline

Bring me your ruse, a rose,
your news,
a more charismatic water.

Tell me your say,
its etymological silk
to finger, a sea
called sea,
a sail called sail,
your *thou art*
or other name for God,
I pray you too catch a wave.

Say me the song this word
once was, un songe,
un mensonge,
a dream caught out.

Mesmerize me,
things being
what they are (stars).

Curious

The way your mouth
says *Owl*, a kiss
of the lips,
apart as we are,
we saints
who dream only of kissing.

Not that I mind
kissing your antlers,
or writing with
this flaming pencil
whatever falls from the sky,
Owl, or brushy, velvety
things so inclined.

Dear Reader

The one who isn't ashamed
of being or doesn't mind
being touched, or touching
like water,
not indifferently,
caressing even a pebble,
the one who touches
an oak with his forehead,
or reads a leaf
with her fingertip,
or a door with his knee
or the air with her mouth,
touching things with her voice,
so they can breathe
and say what they know,
and what she knows.

I Draw a Card

You again, Fish!
Balancing on your head
this time, smiling,
a rose in your mouth,
teacup perched
on your tail—
as if such Christfulness
were an ordinary
cheerful cup,
though I know you worry
for our sake,
and your own, a little.

Nocturne

Urgent to find
a complicit translation,
a dream
not mirroring,
rather attuning to,
or a tuning *of,*
chaos,
a catastrophe
we somehow disarm,
dismantle, rework
the music of,
otherworldly,
oneiric intervals,
is that sound cloud
or tear gas
our own perfume?
Flowering monstrosities,
someone says,
Baudelaire, I guess,
meaning us, and we weep,
as we should,
we all weep at last.

Isabel Dreams Olana

A landscape,
even a face, depends
on having been
dreamed,
dream comes first.

Frederic Church
would've known that,
casting a rectangle
over a meadow,
whitest linen,
a picnic blanket,
I realize, big enough
for a wedding party,
though I'm the only one here.

No doubt, the others
will soon arrive,
carried over
the winding roads
of *the high place*, Eden,
our Olana,
by milk-white donkeys
imported from Syria,
one of the pleasures devised
by Frederic, my husband,

if this be his dream
and I am Isabel.

Isabel,
I lecture myself,
there's nothing to do
but lie down
and wait,
you may as well be dreaming.

I vanish into an owl's call,
"Who cooks for you,
Who cooks for you all?"
The owl vanishes
into the hemlocks,
the hemlocks into history,
snow drifts over me,
silence closes my eyes.

I dream leopards rove
over Persian tiles,
I dream we unbutton
our long, black dresses,
wear nothing
under Bedouin linen,
tulip-like turbans
from Isfahan, a theft,
a pseudo-Levant

of our own invention,
but what makes us dream
our clothes or orchards
or language belong to us?

Fred dreams he's done
with canvas and likenesses,
turns his hand
to roots and branches,
pale green lichen
feeding on granite,
the thick duff
under the hemlocks.
Fixated on shale,
its thousands of layers
of information,
he listens to leaves
and loves his well-house,
his apples and bees,
the weightless red eft
on his palm.
After so much sky,
after Egypt
and all the lurid,
sublime, inexpressible
distances,
he's moved by a drop
at the edge of a leaf,

the small wetness of his wife—
what he knows by touch,
or being touched,
most secret practice
of magic, both
willful and accidental.

Interlude

Among weird things,
a matted hump of fur,
a tiny black shiny carapace,
blooms of orangey lichen
along dead wood,
blooms of pale green
lichen on stone,
nowhere to hide
ourselves,
and no reason to,
I feel small and beautiful,
like a giant at home,
squatting among
the almost bare trees,
my breath added to the
breath of the woods,
the healthful, infectious
sum of things
and me, peeing neatly
between my boots,
my water seeping down
over days and weeks
to a narrow, vernal
stream—just water again,
no one's again.

My friend said a woman
should pee in every story,
and another said
everything will be alright,
is alright now.

I hear a bird calling,
and you, my lookout,
answering,
looking modestly away.

A Dream Caught Out

Under such blue,
mild as Mary's,
what harm
could befall
a falling
child falling
into a lake
or cradle,
a sunlit palace, O
what makes us dream
of drowning in heaven,
what makes us sail
for Jerusalem?

A Sail on Lake St. Clair

We lived in Detroit, not far from the river and Lake St. Clair. We moved from that place when I was five, so I must've been three or four.

We were sailing on a summer afternoon, and I somehow fell overboard, floating on my back for a moment before beginning to descend.

I could hear chatter and laughter from above, and it was lulling, magically so, like the rise and fall of my parents' voices from another room when I was tucked in bed, safe in their nearness, exquisitely free in my aloneness, the sail above me full, billowing, dazzling white, as I lay on my back in the water, the sky a mild, serene blue.

There was no fear at all, sounds growing fainter, barely a murmur, sail still bright but indistinct, a radiance above me, the water over me a transparent sunlit green, the cooler water below holding me, a sensual, even erotic, pleasure, that was also deeply comforting, an experience of absolute trust and bliss.

I forgot the episode for many years, and no one ever spoke of it. At twelve, with more a prefiguring of consciousness than real awareness, for I was vague, drifting from one moment to the next, without much thought or intention, I asked my mother about that day. What had happened? How was I saved? Why did we never mention it?

She was brief, dismissive, telling me only once, firmly, that I had not fallen into Lake St. Clair or any other lake and almost drowned, indeed, we had never been sailing at all. *It was only a dream,* she said, and she sounded as ashamed of my dream as she might have been of letting me drown.

First dream or memory, first embrace—of death or birth or falling in love—the one from which I've never been rescued.

Resembling the Ancestral Types from Which It Has Descended, a Recapitulation

In doubt, say *thou*
to a dream
caught out,
a trembling lake,
alert as a hare, lost
in the wild of your house.

Solve for X or an owl
with a mouthful
of roses,
or ashes of roses,
reverse the order
of operations,
first forgive me,
and all fall down.

Sail or null,
no one there
or here
where you listen
for friend or demon
with only a moon
to see you home,
a dark stone
held up to the light.

And that darkness
you hold
between your lips
is only a word
among others by morning
you find you're able to speak.

Things want to vanish,
be gone, unmarry
like fox-wives
and selkies, go home
to their woods,
real names
and blue mothers.

Unsayable flowers
of flowerville,
dreams, not in
but *of* abeyance,
brief as days,
chanteuses
and troubadours,
ephemeral miracles,
memories, lies,
those sole loves
of humans, the petals
of vast cosmologies.

O, *of*, dear
sleeve of a coat,
trees bare of leaves,
city of silences,
refuge of lies,
the dreams
of an evening
east of a lake,
you mystery
truthful as anyone.

TRUE STORIES

1.

I doubt Socrates said
benevolent moon
or even *restless longing,*
certainly not *tin can.*
Would have asked
Is it true? Can you know?
Might have asked
Isis,
is that your ibis?

2.

May your archetype
coo, a dove-like obsessive
maker of bouquets,
each symbolic blossom
an invitation to tea
in a glass house,
where considering lilies
might take an hour,
an hour at least, an era
of privacy, with such
courtesies petals tremble.

3.

True story, the book
having been left open, plash,
from its pages sprang she,
to scythe she light
without hesitation, lifted
she grails, juggled nails,
bales, codfish gales, tendered
all her questions, she,
on bended knee, befriended he.

4.

Pensive as a rowboat
among lilies she would drift,
or all ceremonious,
hold the thing right firmly,
though uncertain she,
chasing a moth, pointing
there! a Rose,
in case of emergency,
this must be poetry,
where is thy symmetry?
Not lost, only playing, said she.

5.

She chased her ball
to the east, she pliéd,
she shooped
her stick thither, fa la,
skirt and trousers,
she sang, forgive me,
I am a loud child.

6.

Enchantée, nada, nada,
nothing am I if not cross
in a sensual way, I wash
my groceries like grimy children,
never absently. Who cares?
Everyone's little apricot, O
my humble Easter oyster
under a Worm Moon, wait,
did you say *Worm* Moon?
I said Crow, Crust, Sap, Paschal,
Free-for-All, Yes Moon. Well,
I am over it, over that moon,
me, a naif of a worm with no prospects,
no future to speak of, dreamless.

7.

Après un rêve I wake to find this is the only day.
Sirens just as they are serenade me and sorrow
just as it is, and sequins on the asphalt, and ghosts.
Ghosts! So there *was* a day before this one, ours
to squander, a made-up word. *Yestreen I did not know*
how largely I could live. This ordeal-like love.

8.

Never drunk is ever drunk, who knew? Even my hat
is news to me, et j'aime mon chapeau et j'aime mes enfants,
tous les trois, quelle surprise, with three name-day saints,
thirty toes, and thirty questions I don't know the answer to,
how alarming, they're all over me, in my sobriety I feel
like a crystal they shimmy up, and drunk I feel like a green hill
they tumble down over and over but never again, always
anew, and like a pretty, spotted sow I pleasure grunt
and half complain, mais en français, pourquoi pas,
since who knows what language a crystal or a spotted sow
or a never-ending green hill really speaks?

9.

In this story I psychoanalyze myself
and find beauty in restraint
and in excess. I teach myself things
unorthodoxly, become
the embodiment of saudade,
a bizarre and gorgeous nostalgia
for something that never happened.
Like Scheherazade, I see the beauty
of accidents and spectacles, so fearful
I will fall and I do, I see the beauty of fear
and I see the middle ground is the most
extreme, most dangerous place to be,
where you can't escape one thing in the arms of another.

10.

In this story I submit to a riotous music opposite
to the museum-like coolness of a marble forehead,
opposite to beauty itself, even to a curved line
or lines, say your lips saying what can't be said,
whose voice sounds like cedar, tastes like the sun,
speaks its name like a lover deep through the belly,
its one story, its thousand and one.

11.

You clouds of so few words who act like Shakespeare,
I applaud you from my balcony, a standing ovation.
One moon's enough for you, Lorca, and for that
I applaud you, like castanets. Shameless moon and clouds,
shameless Federico! Let's lie down and not do anything
in every octave, let us submit ourselves to every word,
every letter, and to the silences let us devote ourselves.

12.

Three birthday guests for Carlos Lara—a true story.

A dapper man with camera eyes
who sees only what lies under,
hmm, under what? Underwater
undergods, underlings, under skirts,
underthings. He has a cane, tap, tappity,
tap, a rumor in his shoe for you.

A bluish woman sweating honey,
goodness, what a pretty frock,
pretty sticky, pretty smile,
one of the ones that can't help itself,
is it ok to sit on the couch?

An upside-down child in the vestibule
with a little nosegay of waves, aww.
Or is that awful child Carlos, who
once having seen a wave never stopped?

13.

Here you are, Fish,
you birthday wish,
let us lose ourselves
in minutiae, you
in tune Ichthys,
feverish, glamorous
word, never shush.

14.

I was paddling in no rush,
true story, with a broken paddle,
hull studded with arrows,
I almost said sorrows,
my enemies' way of cheering me on,
them singing from both banks,
me in my blue burqa
humming along with the secrets.

15.

A woman sitting with her arms crossed
turned out to be just a break in the weather,
while the one pouring water was just
like a poem, a musical breeze,
and the book in my lap just roared.
I held out a sprig that flowered suddenly,
maybe a remedy, just a suggestion,
the traitor hanging by his heel, like
a chrysalis, forgave himself, just as a crisis
forgives a solution and love forgives card games
and things that just happen, la foi, la loi,
magic and foolishness, the embarrassment of desire.

16.

There's a warehouse of Tarot paraphernalia,
finders-keepers, if you don't mind wading
through the obvious hexagrams, snakes and ladders,
blemished roses and tarnished mirrors, the ear, the antler,
the cross and the teacup, diminishing ice and the
more quotidian couches and spatulas, loaves of bread
and fountain pens, some with books still in them—
thin blue-black or scarlet rinds requiring only a little
water to wet their lips—and a pair of shoes that might
have been sewn by Boehme himself, with mice nesting so
sweetly inside, you can't bring yourself to disturb them.

A LIFE OF ITS OWN

My love for you rises like loaves of bread
inscribed with Hebrew letters,
one every morning for a million years.

My love for you hangs like pluots from witch trees
giving suck to passersby, staining them purple
on moonless nights, without a thought of home.

My love for you plays violins
for an audience of aliens, slender
gentles with goats on their laps.

My love for you sits in my belly
like a green melon, swaying
as I circle the Ka'ba and Maypole.

My love for you returns
relics of the true cross
secretly to the holy land.

My love for you tattoos itself on my ears,
blushing green, pointy as elves'
and now we're invited everywhere.

My love for you crouching under a donkey skin
gives children rides in the park till nightfall,
bathes in the fountain, slumbers in the orangerie.

My love for you learns to pour the tea
into thin porcelain cups in silence,
masters the foil, épée et sabre.

My antlered love for you,
my untoward, uncivil love for you,
smokes opium and takes restless naps.

My love for you balancing
on blue eggshells,
orates unfalteringly.

My love for you picnics nude. Fred
brings the watermelon, Lulu, the cards.
At noon we take shelter under my wedding veil.

My love for you hawks old glass bottles
door to door on a little Greek island,
Santorini maybe, who can remember?

My love for you, resplendent
in pink silk stained under the arms,
loses her fan with the emperor's likeness.

My love for you consorts with otters,
wears my nighty backwards.

IN THE VALLEY OF WONDERMENT

nine invisible paintings by Tamas Panitz

Vespers

Blue cows, majas
couched in blue, blue
flowers, camouflaged
flasks of milk,
repose in the afterlife,
a cool evening
by a crystal fountain,
as if Lorca's rage
and seductive tears
had exhausted themselves
and taken their ease
in a haunted Galician twilight,
the blue-dark Duende's hair
falling over his eyes.

The Simurgh

The plague doctors point
their beaks to God,
Let the one who left us here
speak! But the sky
says nothing.
Let doubt
cure devotion,
and fear cure doubt,
let us be thunderstruck!
Doctors of the unceasing
disease of midnight,
the priests of hankering
linguality advance
and conjure, pointing
their beaks to the stars.
Ourselves is the answer
that falls on their heads.

Gan Eden

It must be the end of time here
in the apple orchard of us
blessed swans and serpents
and kitties who laugh
to find at last we can speak
our own language, though
we still don't get the books
we've written, not even the gist.

No one can see everything yet.
On a distant hill
some naked ciphers
take down a naked cross.
Soon they'll join us,
whoever they are,
bewildered citizens like us,
decent, a little lazy.

Then we'll all head back to the house,
the lovely old mansion of our father,
to eat together and read aloud.

Everyone will be there, and he'll be there too.

Cherchez la Femme

Robert is wrong, the moon's a woman,
O, for orgasm opening her eyes.

It's spring, it's spring! O, the odor
of our ardor, pretty narcissi, almost

too odorous, hours past midnight
when, restless and thirsty, you hear a sound.

There's a woman under the table, no?
And there's your mother's crystal goblet

the only one you haven't broken,
tilted, too close to the edge!

Priests of the Invisible

Me and my friends,
we live for the classics,
Greek myths,
Roman aqueducts,
the Moon.

When we say we *do* things,
we mean we *read* them,
with gravitas.

We clothe ourselves
in greenest silk,
adorn ourselves
with amethysts,
and just stay home
where we belong.

Even that fox
sneaking in like a man
on his hind legs
is pure (as they say)
invention,
though we flap and squawk
as if he were real,
or just look,
embarrassed, away.

According to the Fox

Some can only be seen obliquely,
the tang of their pelts
visible exclusively
in the dark chaotic interior
of green, green's paradise
of terrors, its juice-stained fingers.
Others by dowsing, deceiving, barking,
or waiting, patiently, even till dawn.
Some long to be stolen, devoured,
while others just wish to be seen.
If you can breathe, you're dreaming.

Bay Rum

In this image from the artist's
aftershave period,
he shows forth a scene
of manly things,
the delicate secrets
of Masons
and cardsharps,
the recipes of sailors—
their dreams,
disappointments,
deceptions—and then,
in the morning,
miraculous!
Mended sleeves
and mended valor
for the awful work of being a man.
A pair of aces, sword and shield,
the slap of sunlight, snake eyes.

Still Life

The pear is only itself,
fleshy and sweet,
with a right to be here.
Second, a table,
third, darkness,
fourth, the painter.
He has a right to be here,
alone with a pear in the dark.
He has a right to turn his back on us,
know what he knows, say nothing.

Heraldry

First word rooted in the last,
a post-apocalyptic blossom
trumpeting, Heaven is Here!

Where's here?

In a paradise no paradise,
no one can silence this trumpet or help
this messianic blossom blossom.

FIGURE WITH MEAT

written while listening to Figure with Meat, *music by Grant Tyler*

You can't help a woman
humming—
or whistling the stripped down
melody. Nor can I
not hear her, a surge
in the foreground, a bell
close up, foreplay,
infinite,
infinitesimal.

What meat do you
mean—
the tongue?
A heart
beside itself,
twisting around itself,
breaking—a dance,
falling, a dance.

It becomes
even less—
origin,
first thing—
a swell I can't help
calling feeling—
and can't help feeling,
or calling.

Sound of no thing,
the nothing inside of
a bell, unfurling
rushing train,
tinnitus,
tintinnabula.

Haunted Poe walking
the old streets of Baltimore,
Amity, Mulberry, down
to the harbor,
hectic meat in love.

Horror, the hair of
the back of the neck
erect, to shake—
with (religious) awe.

You can't help
his nerves
or the birds or a river,
can't help our brief span
of attention, a quiver,
a tell-tale heart,
or our fatal lack of
imagination,
our not being able
to get across—

Berryman
tilting,
Celan leaping,
Virginia
drowning herself
in the Ouse,
stones in her pockets,
and April,
who can help April?

I can't help hearing
a siren,
a heartbeat,
the hero's
heart tied to a mast.

The screen goes dark
and I can't help
feeling alarm,
as if I'd been *watching*
the music, and not
merely staring
and *hearing* a heart
on its own—
minimal, animal, alien,
criminal.

The sound of what happens
between the stations,
Christ or Orpheus
tuning in—
because anything
might instruct a person,
anyone befall her.

The heart is a figure
8, meat—
from the root
meaning *wet*,
infinite streaming—
a bowed bell,
the muse, at last.

FRAMEWORK
nine photographs by Flowerville

1.

Of this linen
a supple hand
a seamstress might say,
the way
it falls
and rests, so
pleasant on her.

Woven moonlight
the Gyptians called it,
what would
Swedenborg say?
City, bride, word,
holy They
of the body,
our swaddled
loves. So
did God clothe Jerusalem.

2.

Invisible to us,
stars

at noon,
a hare in snow
and outside the frame
a woman,
hands
in lotus mudra,
beholding
through her lens
herself,
the hare,
if there is one,
round-eyed,
still.

3.

Exceeding white
as snow
are His garments,
so as
no laundress on earth
can whiten them.

And I, the restless, useless laundress.

4.

Equation whose terms
are light and time
in a fugitive minor key,
panic, dispelled
via rhythm and syntax,   .
flowers.

5.

Voice on the verge
of of of
holy
overflow into
a word
winging it,
cloud
is the one
I was looking for,
no, *dove,*
dove is the one.

6.

For my several subjects,
the Oak, my Lord,
mist and lust,
a moon
and a hare
who isn't there.
What else
can I do
with my love for them,
my love for you.

7.

> *With my tongue at rest and my throat silent,*
> *I can sing what I will.*
> —St. Augustine

I, a nothing
more than listening,
late to school,
lost my cello
left my dress
in someone's dream
my body in a glade
somewhere

and there
enact the dromenon,
my body and my alephbet,
with linen for our rituals,
discerning lilies though there is nothing,
sing what I will, it will be spring.

8.

Not every angel
calmly, firmly, kindly
hands a girl a lily,
or after a rest
in the shade of a palm,
after some milk
with bread and honey,
makes an old woman laugh.
One grapples all night,
hard and sweaty, undefeated
even by morning.
Another other lover
burns and tongues
and doves from the body's deep
speechless lust speak.

9.

Time is lost on us, lacustrine,
overbrimming with marvelous fish.
Lovers and swimmers know everything.
Remember the future full of flowers.
We swim in this dream and waltz in others.

MONGOLIAN

for Yuvan

A man with a pasture and no woman,
the moon is his drum.

His horses are stone horses,
cloud horses.

Where does that road go,
the road of a wild dog,
hobbled mule, the road of
a drunken man,
crying man
lying down in the road,
where can such a road go?

His broken heart,
the carcass of a she-goat.
What will become of her child?

Even the wind doesn't know,
keeps asking.
Maybe the stone knows,
maybe the grass.

Someone is counting his goats,
a man is singing his goats
out to pasture
in all that is left of language.

SALITTER

Ecstatic, bittersweet
thou of the sea,
the god in matter,
strewn
grace that praises
whatever it touches,
so do we praise,
do we love,
with our fluencies,
poetries, fleurs
de sel, briny
flowers of Eros,
sal sapientiae,
wise salt, mercurial,
and most difficult
covenant with
our god, the salty one.

CINDERGIRL

for two voices and chorus

Am I here?

Are you my birthday?

Are you dreaming?

Are you my enemy?

Are you wounded?

When I look at you.

Like you this?

Will you stay?

Wish I could tell you.

I could be with you.

Aren't you afraid?

Aren't you afraid?

Only of ever.

How can you tell?

I look in the well. How do you know?

I hurl a thing over.

I've noticed.

Will you be true?

Look in the well . . .

That's only the moon.

all round and shining . . .

Do you promise?

except for what happens.

How will you answer?

Why don't you ask me?

Lady, how are you?

As in the beginning.

How are you called?

By my name.

Where do you live?

In the house with no door.
Call me as you would a fish,
Ishtar,
the Shulamite,
Cinderella.
Call me as you would a sister,
parlous lover, touch me
as you would an ember,
Lucifer,
Eve Before Adam,
Keeps Thy Secrets,
Bewilders the Neighbors.

In what street?

Ocean, dominion, I want to go home
to my sea-serpent mother,
let her scold me and comb my hair.
I'm tired of this donkey-skin,
you can have winter and gravity.
You can have the enchanted rags,
musical dresses, sea-colored

dresses, you can have the mask.
Take the splendid sun shoes!
The famous pair of glass, all yours!
I long only for salt and my own house,
moonlight for a door.

[Meanwhile, fingers are secretly setting
the gates of the city ajar.]

[The gates of the rivers are opened,
and the palace trembles and drowns.]

MAGIC WORDS
for Charlotte the Translator

1.

First thought, *celadon,*
no cup, no vase,
just the cool
vaselike sound of it,
origin, strangely, in *din*
or *clamor,* a tender lover
all in green,
sounding like a king.
His majesty, Céladon!

2.

Speaking of kings,
le roitelet,
the wren flown
leaving only his call,
an ecstatic
rush,
as if air itself
had broken into song.

3.

Spend the day as you would
this coin, on *roitelet*
or *celadon*, a dragon-pitcher
with glistening scales
or a cup as simple
as two cupped hands.

4.

To turn a word
into another, say,
vase to wave—
to translate, weave,
send across, carry over—
at one time *awendan*—
from *wen*, to want, desire,
as in venery.

5.

Venerate Venus,
the alchemist.
If there's time at all,
there's time to change.

6.

Wanting, wander, and wondering,
wend, decant a canticle, vase to ship,
to weave or waver, to move, from
wave to wave to wave.

AS IT IS IN HEAVEN

Since March we've touched
only each other, marrying
over and over.

We begin again like verses
and mornings, ashamed almost
of our luck, the luxe of it.

Sometimes a dream
leads one or the other
into the day, a cloud

or a bird, a well or a mill,
a kiss or a crime or just a feeling
of sadness or menace

left over from having been lost
in a crazy, once familiar city,
something to shake off, dispel,

or the glisten
of a recurring lake,
the illusion of distance

and destination,
thirst, lust,
a place to begin.

We let each other be
or not, a little tea
slops over the rim

of your cup or mine
and the other
takes it personally.

We forget to kiss then kiss,
we marry for love,
agreeing to the sky also,

and the cracked cup,
ruined carpet, pregnant moon,

the postman and the apple tree,
the fox in the yard, the ringing phone,
the table, the bread, the salt.

NEXT MORNING IN A HOLY CITY

Each of us the whole world,
naked and afraid.

But that doesn't last,
there's the sound of a fountain,
very close, a dolphin or lion
we never see
but hear all our days,
or a woman pouring water
endlessly, one vessel into another.

After all, the window's open,
our bodies are warm, the sheets are cool,
one has a book, the other a dream,
how can we stay dead?

We can't stay gone, with a fountain
splashing and each day a fish
who speaks. After all,
we're mostly language
returning to language, spilling
into a world endlessly
grave enough and joyous enough.

LETTERS FROM A HOLY CITY

Over streets that cross themselves
like pilgrims I rove
past houses secreting
the pianoforte, the tragic
perfume of sugar,
linen, lullabies
lost to us.

⁓

Turning right at stones,
left at flames
or jessamine climbing
through wrought iron lyres,
I rove, arriving
at neither moon nor sonnet
nor any answer whatsoever.

⁓

Where else would I be
but under this sky
shining with gods
and beasts who mirror
our condition, ardor.

～

Salt blurs the letters
one by one.
Drifting through alleys
the incense of church
and marsh
fills the post office.
My letters are ruined.
I am ruined.
How shall I send thee?

～

All is wondering, my love.
Let us be wise and never mention
mermaids, divers, reflections,
flirtations with schools of fish
or schools of girls, waiting
for the bus, and all those things
we learned in school and all
that we forgot, in play,
as if everything meant to lead us here,
to this little bed in this little room,
in your chest, a font, oceanic.

~

Sometimes it helps to put things in columns
so mermaids and divers can find each other
lest they wander forever in our dreams
among their reflections and fishy scribbles.

~

Let's meet among the coats and guitars,
along the coast in old armoires,
our limbs entangled
like the beautiful twisted limbs
of live oaks, our own allée in the closet.

~

Let me slip into something more humid,
more like silence, more like a vast starry night
when the walls part like two thoughts
that never were at home with each other,
and I see my chance.

~

Let me start again.
I want you the way the sea
wants herself, returns to herself

the way rivers find their way through marshes
the way one rows through marshes
and tires, and drifts, and dreams of the lover
while hours go by between her thighs
and books write themselves

the way palmettos reach into the sky
with their large, eloquent hands.

⁓

This poem, rowing,
this poem, swimming
up Shem Creek, a dolphin,
this poem, green
Shem Creek itself,
is my own body, tidal,
and your body mirrored,
stiffened with love.

⁓

How many lovers
make love in these alleys,
pressed against the mossy walls,
on the other side of lemon
and fig trees, rich people's gardens,
the sound of their fountains,

angels and lions and green men
with their tongues stuck out,
laughing, stuttering.

⌣

Why name whatever it is we feel?
Why say whose poem,
or what a poem is?

O, do not let us go into battle without a flag.

Quince blossoms, then,
open in winter,
symbols of our aristocracy—
ecstatic Sufis,
bewildered troubadours—
downy fruit perfuming the city.

⌣

Via dark mossy alleys
via the jade eyes of mannequins
I come to the sea,
and she stinks this morning
and so do I
but I try again
and so does she

and we love our failures
and our pencils sprout green ears
like lovers surprising themselves with love.

⁓

I too am afraid of what happens next.
What if my grandmother,
back from the dead,
wants her broken crystal back?
What of the flood, or Pascal's wager?
The catastrophe has already happened.
I hurry to you as green hurries to green
and we take our time as green takes its time.

⁓

Green, how I want you, more than Lorca!

⁓

Whose is this green hand in the sky,
a ripe fruit, Osceola's head,
balancing on the thumb,
the Hierophant, driving out devils,
blessing with silence a sudden white heron.

—

The sin of indigo,
sin of rice,
gold seed rice
from Madagascar,
blue hands, snake bites,
contagion.
How fucking slowly the tongue
that speaks the unspeakable unfurls.
The sin of being able to sleep.

—

Sleep with a mirror under your pillow.
Dreaming of fish means you're pregnant.
A knife under the bed cuts labor in half.
Eat black-eyed peas on New Year's Day.
Blow a red bird a kiss, survive,
never buy shoes for your husband.

—

We have other dead,
other vowels,
we're strangers here
except that we're lovers
naked in the fountain.

Everyone knows
we don't know any better.

⁓

We're bodies under a creamy sky
and can't get our bearings.
Time spreads itself out
over the marsh, thought lapses,
lust turns urgent, obsessive.
When we remember to open our eyes,
salt stings and closes them.

⁓

All is licit. Sunlight
falls like a lover's
undoing hands
over me and over
the barely decipherable
letters inscribed here,
tracing the shape of a wing.

⁓

Seduce, to lead away, astray.
Everything breathes
the pale gold of the marsh grass

the gray of the sky, a soft
almost meaningless the.
Trees live to be as old as prophets,
the sea flows unhinged into Water Street.

—

If a perfume, quince,
rot, honey, tobacco,
if a poem, a slow parlando,
if a church, a fish market.

If the curve of a back,
the arch of a foot,
an angry, itchy bite on the ankle.

—

Hours spent listening
to nothing, addicted
to invisible flowers,
Spanish moss,
a tangled argument,
splendor caught up in it,
evangelical
silence, pleasure,
mercy, all the pleasures,
steeped in brackish water.

～

I've said the lovers,
recounting their dreams,
every meander a tryst.
They lingered here as long as they could.
Now the whole world sways a little.

LADY CHAPEL

She comes early
with her basket of roots.
The work, any work,
takes all day.

Nevertheless, she finds time to clean,
polish the mirrors, fold the linens,
sweep away the trespasses.

She is bereaved, but not for long,
the graveyard is in flower,
knights and bishops,
her own mind a castle,
bird on the sill,
she can't help herself,
the confusion of spring is inside her.

This is her house after all, it seems,
I thought she was the servant of,
floors gleaming, shutters shut,
she is taking a nap, like everyman.
The whole town dozes, even the animals,
chaste and fragrant saints in their dreams.

Our Lady of the Belvedere
is looking with love
over town and country.

She prays for us now
in the measureless
nanosecond of our death,
the haven, the almost chapel
between breathing out
and breathing in, the time
it takes light to take one step.

Our listener of good counsel,
she dignifies the word *our*
with her solemn posture.
She makes *us* possible.

Her hand, her book, her parted robe,
emblems of her openness.

All that's written on earth
or in the sky
she makes valorous
with her gaze,
even a drop, a sigh.

Her glance will catch whatever falls,
careless or bewitched.

Plain language.

Be it unto me.

Remember her joys
as well as her sorrows.

The bathtub Madonna at the end of the street lifts her face to the morning sun, palms held open in compassion, blue veil faded to palest blue, but in afternoon shadow, her porcelain grotto reveals itself a scallop shell, overtly vulvic, as is her own figure, she a sea-born Aphrodite, willful, libidinous, and I a heretic pilgrim, adore her on my way to the Point, a convergence of waters, chaotic, even ecstatic in its resistances, while deep beneath the surface, water sways and acquiesces, as she does, with her same graciousness that exalts the inevitable with surrender, and I am forgiven by her sorrow and by her rapture, and not only me, but all who pass by, who feel guilty and don't know why, we prayers who don't know our prayers.

I'm seven, the year my youngest brother was born, brought home with a touch of jaundice, a golden infant. But in my friend's tent in her backyard, in the dim light, we are far away from our houses and families. We are ourselves.

Pull down your pants and I'll pull down mine, her brother says, and time suspends itself. We are lost together, the boy not much older than me, both of us silenced by the sudden presence of something we will never in all our lives understand.

My friend laughs and the two of us run out into the light, across her yard, into her house. Her mother gives us glasses of juice, purply sweet, and we play in her room with her little horses. We whinny and gallop them, we talk them.

When it's time to go home her mother takes my hand and presses something into my palm, closing my fingers around it. When I open my fist in my own room, there is a small figure of a girl holding open her blue cloak, her head slightly tilted, as if she's listening. She's beautiful and I love her.

I know that she too is a secret and I hide her in my drawer, under the undies. I hold her every day for a few days, then forget to hold her. When I look for her again, she's gone. I know better than to ask who she is or where.

According to Thy Word

Mary, the sound
of her name

sways her, loses her
balance, her book

falls open,
a drift of pollen.

Free to listen
or turn away,

she is her own lute
she tunes accordingly.

How could I imagine
the Lady herself would come instead?

                                        —H.D.

Our lady hails her life
and yours,
conveying to you
her shakti, her juju
conceived of tenderness.

Reanimate the word
lovely for me,
that I may say
how lovely she is,
how stunning
in her confidence.

The alphabet hovers
in her glory,
every letter, at the ready.

A Marian Alphabet

A, as any
girl will tell you,
pomegranate,
seed grenade,
Apple of Granada.
What has she
to do with Apollo,
our Eva, a seed
on her tongue.

B, her belly,
bees in the marigolds,
be it unto me.
Holds every element
in her house.

Christ is only an open mind.

Dea, open
door,
the Delta,
estuarine, uterine.

Everywoman,
her trident
or vulva,

a mermaid
combing her hair.
Etruscan, Eritrean,
Earthling,
lightning in her hair,
her lyre.

Not far, never far.

Grail glyph. Grotto. Glade.
Girl with a book in her lap.

Hi, Helios!
Sun,
salutations.
I greet, I praise
and receive him,
I do.

O Jew,
how you jaw,
you mouth harp,
jujube, apple
that ripens
into a date,
sweet,
and lasts forever.

K, an angel
holding a Lily.
Mirabili dictu,
just like That.

M, the center
of woman, the
Om of her
womb,
the image
descending,
a word
come down
in her, pressing
her open,
and more,
Mem, la mer,
her waters
break and nothing
is as before.

N, a tent,
three sticks, a fire.
She leans on a tree
to labor.

O in itself
an ode
to Our Lady.

A page of cups,
a newsy fish
how you go on,
my darling.

Question,
a begetting
utterance,
water
pouring
from a jar,
U, a jar
overflowing
with nothing,
Q the sound of
blowing soft
across the mouth of U.

R, rapture,
head on fire.
Remember
her roving heart,
her mirth.

Swan, her symbol,
an order of solitude.
I am alone so well
in her presence,
the well of her silence.

Runic T,
the restless
truth, agrees
to be here
among the trees.

Undo, unknot,
unravel. Unfasten
unto me.

Open your eyes
on the verge of Paradise.
Virgin girl-guide,
mediatrix, the Way—
if you can bear her blaze.

Let us draw near
to her blue fire together
to welcome the word,
the wolf, winter.

Nexus,
X, ineluctable
crossing,
catastrophe
of love, my God,
if only a kiss
were enough.

Yeshua,
I am afraid
for you,
for us,
I raise my arms
and cry out—
not why,
Yes.

Z, I zigzag,
resurrect Isis
take refuge
in zero, O
measureless Lady,
virgin plenum
where it begins.

This could be a poem
by Mallarmé,
a throw of the dice,
a memorable crisis
or constellation.
But chance will never abolish
the mind of Guadalupe,
whose every thought
issues a rose,
till her lap, your coat,
the darkness,
are full of them.
Our Lady of the miraculous image,
La Morenita, the brown Lady,
more loved than any other Lady,
speaks to us like a mother
in our own language,
till we are drunk with her.

The Girl Who Knew Everything

At the angel's greeting,
even at the fragrance of the lily,
I think the girl knew everything.

Not that she saw a nailed, crowned body,
as she might now, in our time of
the eye's sovereignty,

but she would have *felt* within her pulse,
the pulse of such a passionate child,
and in the heavy, sweet odor

of the lily, almost
as much meat as flower,
a man's passion.

In the paintings of her listening,
hearing the word, becoming
in that moment pregnant,

I think she knows
and agrees to bear everything,
hear everything, an infant's coos

and wails, and all too soon the lessons
of her young rebbe,
by turns, gentle, fierce, magisterial.

She agrees to hold each word,
keep each word, not in her mind
or in her heart, but in her belly,

hearing also, in her womb,
the agony of a man's body,
and, for a moment, his doubt.

I think she *knew*, at the first quiver
of the air, at the moment of turning
from her book, startled by a lily.

Hearing the word, conceiving of it,
she consented to listening ever after
to each of us, bead by fragrant bead.

The painters make it clear she knows,
even with her child held safe in her lap,
anyone can see, she knows.

Acquiescence

Not as I guessed, with my made-up Latin,
of the nature of water, but from *quiescere,* to rest,

to rest from one's own willing and wanting,
to offer oneself, to agree.

Then what to make of her dancing in the sky,
bare-breasted, a red scarf round her hips

where her power quivers and shakes, a leaping
Mahasiddha, showing us the soles of her bare feet,

her sex, the palms of her hands that beckon
and bless and give this childish world a slap.

Herself absolute, absolutely free,
dancing over our mariologies,
saints and beasts rejoicing.

All images come through her womb,
chaste, promiscuous, motherly, bloodthirsty,

she can turn herself into any emblem
of her virginity: green branch, new moon,

red heifer renewed, a maiden again,
though she has known both God and man

and borne a child and set the church on fire.

Would you say with Boehme that the spiritual body is an oil to be set on fire? I'm thirteen. In the shower I take the smallest steps toward the wall and lean forward till only the tips of my breasts touch the tile. I close my eyes. It occurs to me that I am a virgin now, and that a virgin is nothing like what I've been told, and that what is occurring to me is occurring in language as well as in water, burning like tears, inviolate.

Greenest Branch

Lady, thy paradoxical virginity
has the inconclusive
beauty of a word,
my mind
is not equal to it,
my thought grows hectic
as each proposition
contradicts the rest,
Caesura, tell me
if that is that your name,
or Ampersand.

Lady, in all enclosures
I perceive thy chapel—
between my palms,
in a shadow,
a number,
a fact, a cove, a wave, a tomb,
in a tercet of Dante
or in his crimson cap,
in boat or thurible
or in the month of December,
in the secrecy of a book
or under the dome of the sky,
accept my confusion as devotion.

Lady, I confess thy virginity
and its proof bewilder me.
Broken emeralds mend
themselves, I hear,
when you make love,
like broken hearts or sinners
spared, and branches leaf in fire.
Can you use me in your army,
or in your maiden choir?

As for Rosemarine

for Maggie, Lila, Tracey, Grace, Bridget, and Lydia

As for Rosmarine, I lett it runne all over my garden
walls, not onlie because my bees love it, but because
it is the herb sacred to remembrance, and, therefore,
friendship, thence a sprig of it hath a dumb language.
                                    —Thomas Moore

How sweet our errands are,
from place to holy place,
till all are sacred to us
and all women our mothers,
wives, sisters and daughters.
From porch to porch,
from cradle to altar
to grave, sprig or bundle,
scatter your rosemary here
and here, to keep the thief away.
Braid it into your daughter's hair
that she may remember her Greek.

⁓

Once you've the ocean
in your ear, rosemary grows
wherever you are, healthy and wise,
manly as Christmas trees.

~

Rose of Mary, Rosemarine,
dew of the sea, anciently *anthos*,
simply, *flower*, herb of crowns,
sacred to Aphrodite—
and where it grows a woman rules.

~

Rubbed on the limbs of the Queen of Hungary,
cured her paralysis (13th C).
Likewise, brings faerie from the hedge,
May from April, words from silence.

Our Lady Takes a Dip

Not where you would expect
to find her,
on a hot shore of a salt sea—
she's right here, in the woods
that begin at the end
of your street—
an aperture in a leaf-complected
composition, who turns out to be
something small and naked
curved around itself, pleasantly
shivering, leaves and twigs
stuck to her thighs, a woman
naked, safe in the woods—
if only that were possible.

An aperture in the composition,
as if a painter had left a small shape
unpainted, right at the center—
who else could it be,
as she shakes off our gaze
and all our proposals, like drops of the river.

You can feel the gentle flare of her thought,
her consent, though she wonders when,
maybe where, never the why of it,
but how, how will she know, how will they?

She knows *she* is the why of it,
one of us, we are why.
She settles more trustingly into the light,
into her damp skin, into what is
and will be, forgetting
her husband must be worried,
wondering where she is.

She is called Devel,
Gyptian for God,
who says *I am the mother*
of fair love and fear,
knowing and holy hope,
a window
in the house of truth,
mother of waters,
anchored nowhere,
I draw the lines,
I constellate
the fish and the aleph,
Orion chasing
the sailing sisters,
that flock of doves,
our Pleiades.
I cause
these truths, even death,
to be beautiful,
I bring them down
from the dark of mind
and restore them to brightness,
forth from your very lips.
Appear to me, then,
rovers and dreamers,
as I appear to you.

Our Lady Appears in a Dream

Her pierced heart
a blood-red
emblem of grief,
but closer, a flaming
heart-shaped flask
of some perfume,
rose or myrrh
and closer still, a rose
itself, I can see
is the source of the creek
that flows through our town,
cool and green, brimming with shad
come to spawn in the sweet, local water
for just a few days in April.

Mary, I dreamed you flowed right through me without resistance,
continually, so that everything breathed your perpetual yes.

She's so human someone said *a woman like any other.*

And someone else said *just saying hi to her changes everything.*

Then something settled in us all, like sweetness in a fig, or faith in a
monk, or friendship in a friend.

SESTINA

Each word lives on the cusp
of silence.
Take *Beth*, the word
for B in Hebrew,
meaning *house*,
in which there is no war.

Between your lips there is no war,
tongue lifted to the cusp
of Beth, at peace in her house,
a shell, a world of silence,
as if the restless mind of any Hebrew
would settle in a single word.

There's never been a single word
could tame the human love of war,
whether Greeks or Hebrews
or jealous lovers on the cusp
of hatred, raging in silence,
making two camps of their single house.

Before Beth, Aleph, an ox in the house
of an embrace, a horn, a question-like word
pressed gently (or hard) to the body's silence
that banishes all thought of war
and leaves us swaying on the cusp
of sex, a language ancienter than Hebrew.

I wish I'd studied more Greek and Hebrew,
to pray and orate throughout the house
in such tongues, stuttering on the cusp
of Babel, I'd rejoice in word after alien word.
Bring on pleasure and bring on war!
Distract me from this god-awful silence.

Nothing love I more than silence,
I care not whether Greek or Hebrew,
whether bred from prayer or war,
confusion or fucking or an empty house,
nothing's fiercer than a word
in its solitude, trembling on the cusp.

From the house of language, comes *D'mima*, a rabbinical word
for *bleeding* in Hebrew, and for *silence* also, two words seemingly
   at war.
Though I falter on the cusp of knowing, I know this ancestral
   blood-silence.

DOORS

in memory of Franz Kamin

Through blade-shaped
light-filled crevasse,
through the illusion
chalice, the null

between the profiles of
two lovers,
or any such ruse,
wound, pleasure, calamity
or other heresy hereby
christened *Door,*

but also through such figures as hope,
doubt, despair, hellfire, hilarity,
and through love itself,
as you well know, we go.

Sudden thresholds
along the sunlit boulevard,
doors circulate among us,
and we their music,
their prayers, neither
beseeching
nor exalting, just
being here, playing along,
calling things by their names.

Going through to find
ourselves nowhere,
we dark woods, wild dogs,
grails, betrayals, one terror,
one failure, after another.
Even now we are threshed.
I say *we*, but I alone
don't know the question.
I alone fail to ask.

In the interlude, hips speak to me
in their wisdom, clouds drift through
the pelvic bowl of mind to yours,
whoever you are I've long dreamed of kissing
in dark, recurring hallways, forgive me
for calling you simply *you*.

Thou, a door,
my only prayer.

Feeling along for the edge of a door,
someone's apartment I've lost
the address of, city
in which I am not lost, the body
desiring is not lost, the body
remembering, not lost, a dreaming
body, never lost, speechless
but singing away.

On this hunter's moon I want only to be,
beyond wanting, beyond hunting.

Beyond wanting, a door opens,
less rectangle, more dragon,
she lifts her voice whose flaming letters
describe a splendor solis, the place
we've been looking for all along,
the body of our bodies,
those crises of becoming,
contra naturam, works of art,
angels and swamp creatures,
O, the intelligence of love,
telling us what we've always known
that accidents of light obscure.

So, we can go home
to the sweethearts and gardens
we call heaven,
the sun says it's time
and time is round,
and we can go home.

Or we can squeeze
through smallest vowel,
the o in octopus,
a in clam,
clammed up or clamorous,

scandalous, amorous
moon you can see if you close one eye.
Calm glam little clam. Way up high.

Clam, octopus, you and I
all breathing together in love
with each other, the sea,
its gulls, its boats and words
for clouds, we remember
in reverence, or in fear or mirth,
and in more sorrow than we can say,
though we try, as the parable goes,
it is our nature, this constantly
unfolding enfolding unfolding
tenderness. How could you know
what you cannot know, if that moon,
that pebble, that rickety chair
were not breathing along.

Too weird to think about, the sky
turns indigo, then darker—
even in houses we're uneasy,
drink wine and eat our portion.
Ripe pears please us, we mend
or read our Torahs and Iliads,
make love or revive an argument,
watch a ballgame or play a hand—

and after a while we take off our clothes,
wash ourselves, array ourselves
in old, frayed cotton or nothing
or scraps of silk, and lie down, weirdly,
we all fall down and close our eyes
as if beauty had just pricked her finger,
a giant wing brushes over us all.

On our sides like garden Buddhas
or on our backs, earthlings suspended
in pods over eons, breathing
gently like oceans or children
on our bellies, knees drawn up, thumbs
in our mouths or arms flung out,
legs drooping over the edge of the bed
like tulips, waiting to be born.

And there we meet the fisher king,
the anima mundi and minotaur,
there we're given the magic mirror
and seven-petaled rose, there
we're assigned the impossible task
and there we cry for help, there a stone
falls from the sky, there a boat comes
across the sea to us, there a door opens,
there is a dove who turns into a girl
who plays with our children while we dream.

Franz, I must be dreaming,
because there is no blood,
no wine, no night in our veins
as we carry our threshold
through the mist,
because there is no hour,
no afternoon nor any month
as beautiful, as mystical
as November, only in dreams,
and no one is trying to make love
because we already are,
and everything is,
each twig, caw, step,
though gravity is nothing to us,
we consent, that is all,
we listen as one
and set our door down in the air.

YOU

I fell down a well,
the well was you.

Who is you?
Good question,
well,

every poem has a lover
or other
who is you.

The lover
you thought to be,
you are,

you know it's true
and the poem knows too
that you is you.

~

The you of the poem
is God,
a godlike you,

the poem wants to be
closer to.
You is the truth

and I am Ruth,
the poem who wants
to marry you.

I follow you home,
into the poem.

⁓

I fall for you
into a trance,
I ask you to dance,

play on, poem!

⁓

Who says
I can't say
you, you?

⁓

Who would I be
if not for you
and all the things

I want to do
with you
beneath the apple trees,

you and me as one,
at last, our exile
from each other done,
among the holy apples.

You and me at play
all day. O, you,
is all I have to say.

⁓

I am the fool
who falls into the pool
of you, the poem,

you are the words
who fall into the sky
of I, the birds

who cry,
the why
of the poem

is you, my love,
a dove, O well,
for now, goodbye.

LUMINOUS FAILURES

(In which I essay to answer these questions recently put to me: What concerns does your work address? What is the trajectory of your work over the next year? Please place your work in the context of your field of endeavor. Are you interested in having a community engagement component to your project? If so, what goals do you have in sharing that work with your community?)

true

I would like to say something true about poetry (not particularly my poetry, about which I know so little, less than any reader might) since I have your ear, evanescently, whoever you are, unknown to me, occulted as you are, hidden as a priest in a confessional, a mystic listener. I would like to confess poetry, though nothing I can confess or propose would be as true as a poem itself. And for sure a poem is the better liar.

trajectory

I once dreamed that the poet Jack Spicer threw a spear to me over a crowd of revelers or protesters (and isn't a poem a protest and a revelation) and I caught it in midair, as one catches a word. Jack . . . I call him Jack, since the dead are all equal and all friends . . . Jack was leaning against a tree, squinty-eyed, waiting to see what I would do. I say *the dead, we dead,* because Jack once said, helpfully, *you're dead, now write.*

I wish to write a poem worthy of that spear.

And the immense, impossible Charles Olson said, *the poem is energy transferred from where the poet got it (he will have some several causations), by way of the poem itself to, all the way over to, the reader.*

Those are the trajectories that matter to me.

field

Since you ask, I would place my work in the context of Olson's compositional field, where I place myself out in the Open and breathe whatever comes into being. That is the field of my endeavor.

difficult

Lilies of the field, poems neither toil nor spin, and are not always immediately viable or available, not always socially valuable in any obvious way, though they are ultimately supremely useful. As Williams said, *It is difficult / to get the news from poems / yet men die miserably every day / for lack / of what is found there.*

News that stays news, Pound said.

There are times when I think poems are of no use whatsoever to the world. But what I really think is that poetry somehow finds its way through the hermetic labyrinth of the (world) psyche, renewing our tattered language, making it possible for us lovers and citizens to be braver and more truthful.

being

Does art have the right to exist? is the question posed by the editors of *Caesura,* a young online journal of the arts, and I have wondered not infrequently whether my poems can justify their existence.

Most recently I understand this doubt as part of a larger overarching doubt about whether I myself deserve to exist. I was taught as a girl to be quiet, modest and helpful, not to draw too much attention to myself.

Does every child, her egocentric desires necessarily thwarted, civilized, take on this burden of proof? Are my feelings licit? May I raise my hand? Do I have the right answer? The right to speak? The right to be?

even now

I grew up with brothers, in the perilous, enchanted woods of upstate New York, and in books, especially fairy tales.

In one story, an evil queen turns seven brothers into swans. It is their sister's task to gather nettles from the graveyard at night, and to spin, weave, and sew them into shirts for her brothers, before they must fly north—and this she must do in absolute silence! Only thus can she break the spell and turn the swans back into men. And so she labors night and day, without speaking a word, and the shirts are completed just in time—except for the last sleeve of the last shirt. The youngest brother is left with one arm and one wing. When I write, I am working on that last sleeve.

revelation

Tell the Angel things, said Rilke. There is a secret text hidden in the things of this world, in the glamour of its surfaces, and this text yearns to be heard. The ocean, the beloved, the pebble in your shoe, all clamor for your attention. God wants us to know her real names. We approach with reverence and uncertainty, revulsion, despair, delight, love and hatred, fear and desire. All these are at play in the mirror of the poem, the sacred play of the universe, made visible in the language of things.

failure

The poet Irakli Qolbaia wrote to me recently about not being able to express a certain feeling, *There are no words for it, how luminously they fail!* Later I thought about how the spoken, not the unspoken, fails. Poems are luminous failures, like stars. Poems want to say what can't be said. Or maybe what can only be said continuously, by many voices, singing what can't be spoken. And so, we lift our voices again and again, a great fugue, but in the end, it is the silence after words that is most eloquent. How poetry loves and exalts silence.

The composer Arvo Pärt was writing in his notebook in a churchyard, when a twelve-year-old girl approached him, curious about what he was doing. He explained that he was struggling with his music. *Have you thanked God for your failures?* she asked him. This question is a gift to any artist.

eros

Poetry originates in the body, in the rhythmic, musical nature of the circulatory system and heartbeat, in the ecstasis/enstasis of the breath. Poems are made in bed. Or feet on the floor, ass on the chair, hand moving across the page—air rushes through the etheric larynx and flows (I almost wrote flowers) into the mouth, is shaped by the tongue and lips, speaks.

Ardor is our method, the poet Lou Pam Dick wrote recently.

That's it, really. That could be my whole proposal: *Ardor is our method.* Will you marry me?

Poems are trysts. Poems are amorous, amateurs. They do it, whatever it is they do, for love.

Poems are made in the whorl of the ear, more listening than speaking, all in the mind.

crisis

One thing I have noticed about my poems, with some embarrassment, is that they all seem to be love poems. Are love poems of any use, do they have a right to exist? I am ashamed to be so in love in a world so in crisis, to be so in love *with* a world so in crisis, to meet the terrible crisis of this world with the small crisis of my love. Or are all poems love poems? It's easier to see in some poetries than others, easy to see for example in H.D.'s lyric engagement with myth, body, history. But what about Olson's *Maximus Poems*? Yes, that is a sprawling epic love poem! But you could also say that all poems are political, even if in their rejection of the political, their refusal to address the state's hierarchies and projects. And poems that howl, snarl, and roar may be love poems too.

knife

When I was twenty, I had a lover on the island of Crete. One afternoon, I visited with his sister, who was fluent in English, though she rarely had the chance to speak it. We'd been sitting in her kitchen conversing in English for about fifteen minutes when her four-year-old son grabbed a knife from the table and charged at me. What had happened? He was terrified that his mother was speaking—and that he could not understand a word she said.

That's why so many people run away from poetry, or even attack it. It sounds like the language we use every day to make grocery lists and arrange meetings, but suddenly we don't *understand* what's being said, we cannot understand our *mother-tongue*, and this is fundamentally disorienting and frightening. Even the poetry closest to ordinary speech makes something else of it, something more intense, meaningful, odd.

People have become accustomed to abstraction in painting, music, film, dance, but still want to *understand* language, even the language of poetry, as a kind of currency, in its most materialistic, utilitarian manifestations. Readers ask, what does the poem mean, what does it *really* mean, what's it *about*? As if the text were a screen hiding the real poem, the real world.

Two words on a page create meaning, relationship. One, even. It's just that meaning isn't where you expect to find it—it's not up the poem's sleeve, it's hidden in plain sight, in *the experience* of the poem, the ordeal of the poem, in the reader's response, in his feeling life, in her intellect, *in their body*. That sounds naive, but it isn't.

The meaning of the poem *is* all the naked, unruly events (swoons, images, associations, a change in one's pulse) as they arise and vanish (or persist, evolve, *change one's mind*) in response to the crisis of the poem, that is, in response to the poem's refusal to be meaningful.

... the withdrawal of meaning by which meaning happens, Jean-Luc Nancy says of philosophy, but I think that for him philosophy aspires to the condition of poetry.

roots

When we were children, my father would get drunk and read Shakespeare, Whitman and Poe aloud. When I was thirteen, he went on a business trip to NYC and brought me back a slim New Directions paperback of Lorca's selected poems. Those poems are still in my ear.

I left home at seventeen and wandered into Bard College at eighteen. I sat in on a course taught by Robert Kelly, whose poems still inspire mine, and in the very first class he read Robert Creeley's astonishing poem, *The Door*. Thus I staggered through Creeley's door, all the way through to poetry, to the writing of it.

Through Creeley, I found Olson and Duncan, one of my poetry heroes ever after, and via Duncan, H.D., a revelation to me, a poetry mother and fearless poet warrior.

A few days after that first class, I brought that great barbarossa of a poet, Kelly, a poem, an awful poem, and he said *bring more* and gave me a cookie, for the poems not yet written.

ours

I find it odd to say *my poems*. They are not mine, just as my daughter is not mine, my husband not mine.

Robert Duncan argued steadfastly that his work was derivative. Once, defining his work, he simply listed the names of forty-three other poets, dead and alive. I too am aware that I write within a constellation, a web, a hive.

The work of other poets is vital to me. Freed from imagining my work is my own, I rejoice in the poetries of others and can only hope that their various formal and intangible suavities and heresies rub off on me, stain me with their light.

The best poems make me want to write back. Our texts nudge and prod, arouse, infuriate, contradict and slay each other, catch fire from each other, catch each other's diseases, and sometimes heal them.

good poem/bad poem

Rumors, scandals and oracles, good poems resist preconceived ideas or placing themselves in context, or any knowledge they do not discover for themselves in the course of becoming. They are not interested in what we already know or expect to hear; they do not comfort us in that way, though they may comfort us in other ways, more profoundly than any mother.

Language dreaming, good poems wonder, with gravity, and levity. They are curious. They guess, heroically.

They are bazaars, churches, dark alleys and quiet glades, into which the unsayable is spoken and from which it issues.

Good poems are not afraid of beauty, however fierce, the beauty of, say, crow or caw.

Good poems terrify, incite and caress us, rejoice and pray with us, now and in the hour of our death.

A good poem is both a devotion and a heresy.

Like traditional Chinese medicine, good poems want to bring you closer to your destiny, and thus may provoke an ordeal, a crisis.

There are many kinds of bad poems, but the worst thing a poem can do is to make you feel virtuous, to assure you that you are firmly on the right side of something. Run from those.

A good poem does not make you feel virtuous, it makes you feel terribly human—tender, doubtful, sometimes fearful and sometimes brave, sorrowful or mirthful, maybe prayerful, in love, full of longing, or just being—lost in the wild, an ecstatic nobody.

NOTES

The verse of Paul Celan's poem serving as an epigraph to this volume is translated by Pierre Joris in *Memory Rose into Threshold Speech*. Farrar Strauss Giroux, 2020.

Madame Lulu, channeled in an epigraph to this volume, was created by Sarah Falkner in *Madame Lulu's Book of Fate: An Interpretive Guide to Kahn/Selesnick's Carnival at the End of the World Tarot Deck*. Truppe Fledermaus, 2018. http://kahnselesnick.biz/ + http://sarahfalkner.com/ Some of the images of a "A Sail on Lake St. Clair," "True Stories," and "A Life of Its Own" were inspired by the imagery of that deck.

Yestreen is an archaic contraction of *yesterday evening*. Looking up its history, I found theses lovely lines by one Bishop Coxe: *Yestreen I did not know/How largely I could live.*

You may find the visible paintings of Tamas Panitz on Instagram. The title of *In the Valley of Wonderment* references the Persian poem *Conference of the Birds,* by Sufi poet Attar of Nishapur. *Priests of the Invisible* references Wallace Stevens's *the poet is the priest of the invisible,* from *Opus Posthumous*, "Adagia."

The poems of *Framework* respond to the images of Flowerville. Her photographs and photograms may be found on Flickr. There is also a reference to her book, *Flowers of Abeyance*, in the poem sequence "A Sail on Lake St. Clair."

Cindergirl is a convergence of Cinderellas and other archetypes. Several lines are quotes from traditional fairy tales; one line is Thomas Wyatt's; the two texts in brackets that conclude the poem are from *Acts of Thomas*, and from the Old Testament, *Book of Nahum*.

Holy City is a nickname for Charleston, South Carolina. *Next Morning in a Holy City* quotes Jean-Luc Nancy's *The Gravity of Thought*: "The weight of thought means that the world is grave enough by itself, without any other consideration. Which also means: joyous enough."

O do not let us go into battle without a flag is an inscription on the Jasper Monument in Charleston, South Carolina's White Point Garden, commemorating the 1776 Battle of Sullivan's Island, in which Colonel William Moultrie and 400 Continental soldiers defended the uncompleted Fort Sullivan against the British. The fort, at the mouth of Charleston Harbor, was later completed and renamed Fort Moultrie.

The betrayal of Osceola, the Seminole leader who resisted "Indian Removal" during the Trail of Tears, and his imprisonment and death in 1838 at Fort Moultrie, was brought to my attention by Celia Bland (text) and Cameron Seglias (images) in their collaboration, *Shooting Script: Brazen Jackson, episodes 1–13*. A video reading of some episodes of the poem cycle may be found here: www.youtube.com/watch?v=8diRVDODlIQ

The poem beginning *Our Lady Hails Her Life*, in the sequence *Lady Chapel*, bows in homage to H.D.'s *Tribute to the Angels*.

Doors recalls an afternoon spent with poet/filmmaker Franz Kamin and some of his friends, wandering through the woods carrying an old door. Franz would set up the door and film whatever happened next, for his project, *Concert of Doors*. The imagery of the lines *there is a dove who turns into a girl/who plays with our children while we dream* is drawn from Carl Jung's account of one of his own dreams.

The poem *You* alludes to goings-on under apple trees—according to Kabbalistic lore, God so loved human intimacy that They caused apple orchards to spring up in the sand to shelter picnicking lovers. *The Field of Holy Apple*s is another name of the Shekhinah.

ACKNOWLEDGMENTS

Some of the poems in this volume were published as earlier versions in the following print and online journals and pamphlets: *Among the Neighbors, Blazing Stadium, Caesura, Columba, Dispatches from the Poetry Wars,* and *NoMaterialism.* I'm grateful to the editors of those publications—Michael Boughn, Austin Carder, Lila Dunlap, Whit Griffin, Kent Johnson, Emily Tristan Jones, Carlos Lara, Edric Mesmer, Tamas Panitz, and Chloe Bliss Snyder.

I'm grateful to these friends too, for their encouragement and excellent ears: Maria Black, Mary Caponegro, Peter Cole, Lisa Fishman, Michael Ives, Robert Kelly, Charlotte Mandell, Joel Newberger, Irakli Qolbaia, and Maggie Zavgren.

I am ever grateful to my first reader, Larry Chernicoff.

I would like to thank Austin Carder and Caesura, Robert Kelly, Kimberly Lyons and Lunar Chandelier Press, Mary Newell, Monty Reid and the Ottawa Versefest, Phong Bui and company at the *Brooklyn Rail,* and George Quasha, for opportunities to read the work aloud.

Deepest thanks to John Yau and Black Square Editions for giving these poems a place to be found. I had thought to leave them on trains and buses.

ABOUT THE AUTHOR

Billie Chernicoff was born left-handed in Detroit. Now she lives in a blue house one street away from the Hudson River, great outstretched arm of the Atlantic. Her garden is her fifth garden. *Minor Secrets* is her fifth book of poetry.

Black Square Editions was started in 1999 with the intention of publishing translations of little-known books by well-known poets and fiction writers, as well as the work of emerging and established authors. After twenty-three years, we are still proceeding book by book.

Black Square Editions—a subsidiary of Off the Park Press, Inc, a tax-exempt (501c3) nonprofit organization—would like to thank the following for their support.

Tim Barry
Robert Bunker
Catherine Kehoe
Taylor Moore
Goldman Sachs
Pittsburgh Foundation Grant
Miles McEnery Gallery (New York, New York)
I.M. of Emily Mason & Wolf Kahn
Galerie Lelong & Co. (Paris, France)
Bernard Jacobson Gallery (London, England)
Saturnalia Books
& Anonymous Donors

BLACK SQUARE EDITIONS

Richard Anders *The Footprints of One Who Has Not Stepped Forth* (trans. Andrew Joron)

Andrea Applebee *Aletheia*

Eve Aschheim and Chris Daubert *Episodes with Wayne Thiebaud: Interviews*

Eve Aschheim *Eve Aschheim: Recent Work*

Anselm Berrigan *Pregrets*

Garrett Caples *The Garrett Caples Reader*

Billie Chernicoff *Minor Secrets*

Marcel Cohen *Walls (Anamneses)* (trans. Brian Evenson and Joanna Howard)

Lynn Crawford *Fortification Resort*

Lynn Crawford *Simply Separate People, Two*

Thomas Devaney *You Are the Battery*

Ming Di (Editor) *New Poetry from China: 1917–2017* (trans. various)

Joseph Donahue *Infinite Criteria*

Joseph Donahue *Red Flash on a Black Field*

Rachel Blau DuPlessis *Late Work*

Marcella Durand *To husband is to tender*

Rosalyn Drexler *To Smithereens*

Brian Evenson *Dark Property*

Serge Fauchereau *Complete Fiction* (trans. John Ashbery and Ron Padgett)

Jean Frémon *Painting* (trans. Brian Evenson)

Jean Frémon *The Paradoxes of Robert Ryman* (trans. Brian Evenson)

Vicente Gerbasi *The Portable Gerbasi* (trans. Guillermo Parra)

Ludwig Hohl *Ascent* (trans. Donna Stonecipher)

Isabelle Baladine Howald *phantomb* (trans. Eléna Rivera)

Philippe Jaccottet *Ponge, Pastures, Prairies* (trans. John Taylor)

Ann Jäderlund *Which once had been meadow* (trans. Johannes Göransson)

Franck André Jamme *Extracts from the Life of a Beetle* (trans. Michael Tweed)

Franck André Jamme *Another Silent Attack* (trans. Michael Tweed)

Franck André Jamme *The Recitation of Forgetting* (trans. John Ashbery)

Andrew Joron *Fathom*

Andrew Joron *OO*

Karl Larsson *FORM/FORCE* (trans. Jennifer Hayashida)

Hervé Le Tellier *Atlas Inutilis* (trans. Cole Swensen)

Eugene Lim *The Strangers*

Michael Leong *Cutting Time with a Knife*

Michael Leong *Words on Edge*

Gary Lutz *I Looked Alive*

Michèle Métail *Earth's Horizons: Panorama* (trans. Marcella Durand)

Michèle Métail *Identikits* (trans. Philip Terry)

Albert Mobilio *Me with Animal Towering*

Albert Mobilio *Touch Wood*

Albert Mobilio *Games & Stunts*

Albert Mobilio *Same Faces*

Pascalle Monnier *Bayart* (trans. Cole Swensen)

Christopher Nealon *The Joyous Age*

María Negroni *Berlin Interlude* (trans. Michelle Gil-Montero)

Doug Nufer *Never Again*

John Olson *Echo Regime*

John Olson *Free Stream Velocity*

Eva Kristina Olsson *The Angelgreen Sacrament* (trans. Johannes Göransson)

Juan Sánchez Peláez *Air on the Air: Selected Poems* (trans. Guillermo Parra)

Véronique Pittolo *Hero* (trans. Laura Mullen)

Pierre Reverdy *Prose Poems* (trans. Ron Padgett)

Pierre Reverdy *Haunted House* (trans. John Ashbery)

Pierre Reverdy *The Song of the Dead* (trans. Dan Bellm)

Pierre Reverdy *Georges Braque: A Methodical Adventure* (trans. Andrew Joron and Rose Vekony)

Valérie-Catherine Richez *THIS NOWHERE WHERE*

Barry Schwabsky *Book Left Open in the Rain*

Barry Schwabsky *Feelings of And*

Barry Schwabsky *Heretics of Language*

Barry Schwabsky *Trembling Hand Equilibrium*

Jeremy Sigler *Crackpot*

Jørn H. Sværen *Queen of England* (trans. Jørn H. Sværen)

Genya Turovskaya *The Breathing Body of This Thought*

Matvei Yankelevich *Some Worlds for Dr. Vogt*